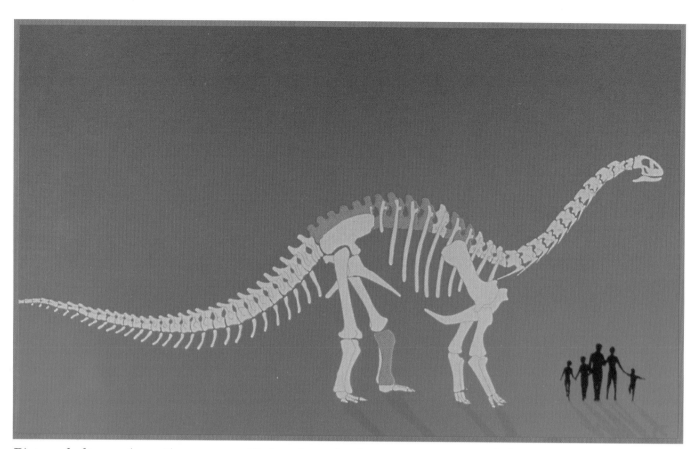

Pictured above: *Argentinosaurus* • Pictured on the front cover—at top (left to right): *Corythosaurus*, *Mussaurus*, *Troodon*, and *Protoceratops*; bottom: *Tyrannosaurus* • Pictured on the title page: *Seismosaurus*

Dinosaurs

by
Rebecca L. Grambo

Scientific consultants:

Mark A. Norell
Chair of the
Division of Paleontology
American Museum of
Natural History

and

Carl Mehling
Scientific Assistant
Department of Herpetology
American Museum of
Natural History

kidsbooks
Incorporated

Introduction

Dinosaurs have fascinated generations of humans—from 1824, when the first dinosaur was named (*Megalosaurus*), to this very minute. Perhaps the most amazing thing about dinosaurs is how long they dominated life on Earth—more than 160 million years! They fascinate most of us, it seems, for two other reasons as well: their huge size and the fact that they are extinct, gone forever. But neither of these things tells the whole story.

Some dinosaurs were huge (tall enough to peek into a fourth-story window!), but others were no larger than a modern-day chicken. As for extinction, most dinosaurs did die out 65 million years ago. A few remain on Earth, however, and you see them every day—birds, which many experts consider to be dinosaurs, live among us still.

This book will introduce you to many extinct dinosaurs, as well as other animals long gone but not forgotten. Dinosaurs tend to have very long names, so we've given you a guide to pronouncing tough words (in parentheses). There is also a glossary at the back of the book, providing explanations of terms that might be unfamiliar.

Are you ready to enter the world of dinosaurs?

Dinosaurs, large and small: *Diplodocus* (dih-PLOH-duh-kus), a 90-foot-long plant-eater of the Jurassic Period, and *Deinonychus* (dye-NON-ih-kus), a 13-foot-long meat-eater of the Cretaceous Period.

Contents

Fossils

How do we know so much about animal and plant life that are not around any more? The answers lie in fossils.

Fossils are evidence of ancient living things. By studying them, paleontologists (*see glossary*) can learn about dinosaurs and other life from long ago.

Fossils are not just bones. Many things can be fossilized, including teeth, wood, shells, and footprints, or faint impressions of skin, feathers, or leaves.

How does something become a fossil? Usually, it happens like this:

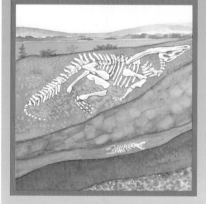

Parasaurolophus

Becoming a Fossil

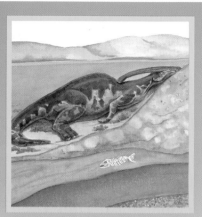

The dead animal sinks to the bottom of a lake, river, or sea. Some of its body rots or is eaten.

Whatever is left of the animal (usually, a skeleton) becomes covered with fine mud.

A lot of time passes. Gradually, the original skeleton is replaced with minerals and becomes part of the surrounding rock.

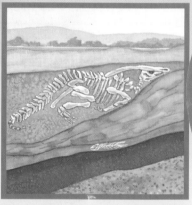

More time passes. The water dries up, or rocks are pushed to the surface. Wind and weather wear down the rock until the fossil is close enough to the surface to be found.

8

They Weren't All Dinosaurs

Rhamphorhynchus, a flying reptile of dinosaur times, was not a dinosaur.

Mastodonsaurus, one of the largest amphibians that ever lived, lived in dinosaur times but was not a dinosaur.

Dinosaurs were reptiles that lived on Earth in prehistoric times. Most of them died out about 65 million years ago, but they dominated Earth for more than 160 million years before that! More than 150 species of dinosaur lived during the Mesozoic Period (not all at the same time). Not every now-extinct reptile that lived at that time was a dinosaur. Pterosaurs, such as the *Rhamphorhynchus* above, were not dinosaurs. Neither were many reptiles that swam in lakes or seas. Most dinosaurs were land animals, but nondinosaur reptiles lived on land, too.

Elasmosaurus, a large sea reptile that lived in dinosaur times, was not a dinosaur.

DID YOU KNOW . . . ?
The word *dinosaur* means "fearfully great lizard."

9

Dinosaur Types

Dinosaurs are divided into two main groups, based on their hip bones. Saurischian (saw-RISH-ee-un) dinosaurs have hips that look sort of like a lizard's. Ornithischian (or-nuh-THISH-ee-un) dinosaurs have hips that look more like a bird's.

SAURISCHIANS
(LIZARD-HIPPED DINOSAURS)

There are two main types of saurischians.

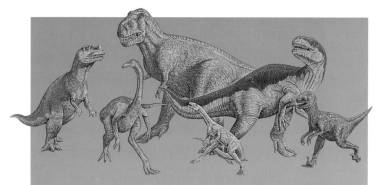

Left to right: *Ceratosaurus, Ornithomimus, Tyrannosaurus, Coelophysis, Allosaurus,* and *Deinonychus.*

THEROPODS

(The name means "beast-footed.")

• most ate meat; some may have eaten meat and fruit
• most had sharp teeth and claws (though some were toothless)
• most walked on strong back legs; were swift runners

SAUROPODS

(The name means "lizard-footed.")

• ate plants
• had heavy bodies, long necks and tails, and short, stumpy legs
• walked on four legs

Left to right: *Cetiosaurus, Camarasaurus, Opisthocoelicaudia, Brachiosaurus, Mamenchisaurus,* and *Diplodocus.*

ORNITHISCHIANS
(BIRD-HIPPED DINOSAURS)
There are three main types of ornithischians.

ORNITHOPODS
(The name means "bird-footed"—though few had feet that look like a bird's.)
- ate plants
- probably stood on their back legs as well as all four
- had beaklike mouths
- had three or four clawed toes

From left to right: *Ouranosaurus, Iguanodon, Heterodontosaurus, Parasaurolophus,* and *Hypsilophodon.*

From left to right: *Psittacosaurus,* believed to be an ancestor of ceratopians; *Triceratops, Styracosaurus, Torosaurus, Pentaceratops,* and *Protoceratops.*

CERATOPIANS
(The name means "horned faces.")
- ate plants
- most had horns on their heads and faces
- had heavy, bulky bodies and walked on four feet
- had frill or shieldlike crest on their necks

ANKYLOSAURIA
(The name means "fused lizards.")
- ate plants
- walked on four legs
- had bony plates and spikes protecting their bodies
- two types: ankylosaurs (wide head, club on end of tail) and nodosaurs (narrow head, sideways-pointing spikes, no club on tail)

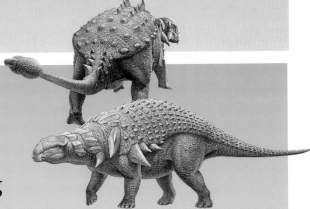

Top to bottom: *Euoplocephalus,* an ankylosaur, and *Edmontonia,* a nodosaur.

11

Geological Time Chart
What Happened When

ERA	PERIOD	YEARS AGO*	AGE	IMPORTANT EVENTS
CENOZOIC	**Quaternary:** Holocene Epoch	10,000 years ago to present		Cities appear (about 5,000 years ago).
	Pleistocene Epoch	1.65 mya to 10,000 years ago		Anatomically modern humans appear (about 200,000 years ago); cave painters (about 50,000 years ago).
	Tertiary: Pliocene Epoch	5 to 1.65 mya	Age of MAMMALS	Human ancestors (*Australopithecus*) appear (about 4 mya).
	Miocene Epoch	23 to 5 mya		Grazing mammals become more widespread.
	Oligocene Epoch	35 to 23 mya		Many mammals start evolving into modern forms.
	Eocene Epoch	57 to 35 mya		The Himalaya mountains start to rise when India crashes into Asia (about 45 mya).
	Paleocene Epoch	65 to 57 mya		Many new kinds of mammals evolve.
MESOZOIC	Cretaceous	145 to 65 mya		Dinosaurs dominate the land; many new, exotic forms. First flowering plants. At the end of this period, dinosaurs (except birds), pterosaurs, marine reptiles, and many other animals and plants become extinct.
	Jurassic	208 to 145 mya	Age of REPTILES	Pliosaurs appear: Dinosaurs dominate the land; mammals remain small. Appearance of first birds.
	Triassic	245 to 208 mya		The first dinosaurs appear; so do frogs, turtles, crocodiles, pterosaurs, and the first mammals. Plesiosaurs appear.

Era	Period	Time	Age	Description
PALEOZOIC	Permian	290 to 245 mya		Reptiles become the dominant animals on land. Time of the sailfin reptiles. This period ends with the greatest extinction event in Earth's history.
	Carboniferous	362 to 290 mya	Age of AMPHIBIANS	Time of great forests. (Over millions of years, their remains become coal.) The first winged insects appear. Late in this period, the first reptiles evolve.
	Devonian	408 to 362 mya	Age of FISHES	Sharks appear; so do armored fish. The first forests evolve; trees grow up to 30 feet tall. Near the end of this period, the first seed-producing plants appear, and the first amphibians evolve from fish.
	Silurian	440 to 408 mya		Plants begin to grow on land. The first jawed fish appear. There are fish in fresh-water as well as in oceans. Millipedes and scorpions move on to land.
	Ordovician	510 to 440 mya		First coral reefs appear. There also are nautiloids (NAW-till-oydz), squidlike creatures with long, pointy or coiled shells.
	Cambrian	570 to 510 mya		Many kinds of creatures appear in the oceans, including sponges, starfish, sea urchins. Also, the first shelled animals—clamlike brachiopods (BRAK-ee-oh-podz), and trilobites (TRY-loh-bites) that crawl over the sea floor. Fish appear—the first creatures with backbones.
Precambrian		4.5 bya to 570 mya		Earth forms (around 4.5 bya). Life on Earth begins (around 3.8 bya).

*bya = billions of years ago ● mya = millions of years ago

Dinosaur Times

Dino-saurs have lived on Earth for 200 million years—much longer than humans have. But not all dinosaur species (kinds) lived at the same time. Many different species came and went during those years.

Allosaurus

Allosaurus (AL-uh-SORE-us) and *Tyrannosaurus* (ty-RAN-uh-SORE-us) were both massive meat-eaters. But *Allosaurus* lived about as many years before *Tyrannosaurus* as *Tyrannosaurus* lived before us humans. A *Tyrannosaurus* may even have stubbed its toe on 70-million-year-old fossilized *Allosaurus* bones sticking out of the ground!

Tyrannosaurus

14

How much longer were dinosaurs on Earth than humans? If you look at your arm and imagine that the very first life on Earth happened at your shoulder, dinosaurs began near your elbow and dominated Earth to your wrist. Humans have been here only for the bit of time represented by the tip of one of your fingernails!

DID YOU KNOW . . . ? Dinosaurs have lived all over the planet. Dinosaur bones have been found on every continent—including Antarctica. Dinosaurs lived in swamps, forests, and very dry areas.

Before the Dinosaurs

Fossil of a Precambrian jellyfish

Dinosaurs were not the first animals on Earth. Animals living in the Precambrian had very few hard parts, such as bones or shells, that make good fossils. Only a few places on Earth show a record of life from this early time.

In a fossil-rich area of Canada called the Burgess Shale, rocks are as much as 530 million years old! Among the fossils in these rocks are some really weird-looking Cambrian animals. One is a 25-inch-long legless beast with two eyes on stalks. Another is a five-eyed wormlike animal.

16

Some trilobites (TRY-loh-bites) survived until the end of the Permian Period, but they were at their peak in the Ordovician. Up to 27 inches long, the trilobite's name comes from the fact that its body is divided length-wise into three parts. (*Tri* means "three"; *lobe* means "part.") Trilobites are the earliest fossil animals to show well-developed eyes.

A trilobite crawls at the bottom center of this Ordovician sea scene.

Giant sea-scorpions, or eurypterids (yur-IPP-tur-idz), scuttled across muddy Silurian sea floors. Some grew to longer than five feet! Some scorpions had moved onto land earlier—they probably were distant relatives of the eurypterids.

Eurypterid fossils

Ichthyostega

Ichthyostega (ICK-thee-oh-STEG-uh), from the Late Devonian Period, may have been the first four-legged animal to walk on land. It was an amphibian—an animal that can live on land but must lay its eggs in water so they don't dry out. *Ichthyostega* probably spent a lot of time hunting in the water.

Dunkleosteus

Ammonite

There were some new hunters in Carboniferous seas. Ammonites (AM-uh-nites) looked a bit like squid stuffed into big snail shells. They ate trilobites and other shellfish.

18

Dunkleosteus (left) was one of the largest ocean predators of the Late Devonian Period. It grew close to 20 feet long! It was heavily armored with bony plates that shielded its head, sides, and upper back. Its sharp dental plates worked like teeth to grind up its prey.

DID YOU KNOW . . . ?
Reptiles first appeared in the Late Carboniferous Period. Their eggs had a hard protective shell, so reptiles could do something that amphibians could not: lay their eggs on land.

At the end of the Carboniferous Period, there were some very big insects around. One, very much like a dragonfly, had a wingspan of up to 2.5 feet. There was also a centipedelike creature that grew up to 6.5 feet long, and a spider about 14 inches wide!

Moschops

The plant-eating *Moschops* (MAHS-kops) may look pretty tame, but don't let that fool you. *Moschops* had powerful legs and very thick skull bones on the top of its head. This reptile of the Permian Period probably used its thick skull to head-butt other *Moschops*, the way some modern-day goats do.

Two sailfin reptiles: carnivore *Dimetrodon* (upper left) and herbivore *Edaphosaurus* (lower right).

Imagine a seashore with 10-foot-long, fin-backed reptiles soaking up the sun! *Dimetrodon* (dye-MEET-row-don), a meat-eater, and plant-eating *Edaphosaurus* (ee-DAF-uh-SORE-us) had fins supported by long spines growing from their back-bones. These reptiles died out millions of years before the first dinosaurs appeared.

Mesosaurus

Mesosaurus (left), the oldest known aquatic (water-dwelling) reptile, lived in shallow, coastal waters of South America and Africa during the Permian Period.

About three feet long, it had teeth, but used them to sift food from the water, not to chew.

Some of the plants and animals found in Permian seas.

This fossil of a reptile that lived during the Late Permian was found in Texas.

DID YOU KNOW . . . ?

The end of the Permian Period was marked by one of the biggest extinction events in Earth's history! As much as 90 percent of life may have been wiped out. This may have helped clear the way for the rise of the dinosaurs.

Life in the Triassic

By the end of the Permian Period, the continents had bunched together (see map, far right) into a supercontinent called Pangaea (pan-JEE-uh). But by the end of the Triassic, Pangaea was breaking up —very slowly. All over the world, the climate was warmer than it is today—there was less difference in temperature between the poles and the equator.

Some plants from this scene of 220 million years ago still exist, including conifers, ginkgoes, ferns, and palm-like cycads.

Left to right: *Plateosaurus*, *Coelophysis*, and *Lystrosaurus*.

22

Triassic seas were filled with hunters like the ichthyosaur (IK-thee-oh-sore), a marine reptile.

Erythrosuchus (uh-RITH-rah-soo-kus) and *Euparkeria* (yoo-par-KEE-ree-uh) were meat-eating reptiles of the Early Triassic. They weren't dinosaurs, but probably were dinosaur ancestors. In its day, *Erythrosuchus* was the biggest predator on land. You can see why some plant-eaters from this time had body armor!

Erythrosuchus

Euparkeria

Plateosaurus (PLAT-ee-uh-sore-us) is a commonly found Late Triassic fossil. One of the first large dinosaurs, it grew to 26 feet long. ● **Coelophysis** (SEEL-uh-FYE-sis) may be the best-known of the oldest dinosaurs, because so many of its fossilized remains have been found. It arose in the Late Triassic. Its size ranged from just over 3 feet to 10 feet in length. ● **Lystrosaurus** (LIS-trah-sore-us) was a reptile, not a dinosaur. It was a plant-eater that probably used its small tusks to defend itself against meat-eaters. It was a little over 3 feet long.

Triassic Plant-eaters

The first plant-eating dinosaurs appeared during the Triassic. Some of them belonged to a group known as prosauropods (proh-SORE-uh-podz), because they look a little like sauropods, a later dinosaur group that included *Apatosaurus* (uh-PAT-uh-SORE-us). Scientists think that these groups had a common ancestor.

The biggest and heaviest prosauropod discovered so far is the 40-foot-long *Melanosaurus* (muh-LAN-oh-SORE-us), found in South Africa.

An adult *Mussaurus*

The tiny skeleton of a baby *Mussaurus* (muh-SORE-us) is one of the smallest dinosaur skeletons (except for those still in eggs) yet found. Its skull is just over an inch long and the entire skeleton fits into a man's cupped hands. *Mussaurus*, found in present-day Argentina, was a prosauropod that lived about 215 million years ago. Its name means "mouse lizard."

We have only a few bones from the prosauropod *Agrosaurus* (AG-roh-SORE-us). In 1844, an explorer from a British ship went ashore in Australia and did some digging around. He found *Agrosaurus* bones—the first Australian dinosaur fossils found and the only ones from the Triassic Period.

A *Plateosaurus* herd caught in a flash flood

Did *Plateosaurus* travel in herds? The remains of many *Plateosaurus* were found in one spot. That could mean that something killed a herd all at once—or that bones from different times and places were swept into one place by heavy rains.

> **WORDS FOR THE WISE**
> The name of this group of dinosaurs—prosauropods—describes them quite well! *Pro-* means "earlier than," *sauros* means "lizard," and *-pod* means "foot."

Little *Pisanosaurus* hides from a larger meat-eater.

Pisanosaurus (pye-SAN-uh-SORE-us) is the oldest known member of the ornithischian (bird-hipped) dinosaur group. It lived about 225 million years ago, in what is now Argentina. Scientists guess that it was probably a fast, two-legged runner.

Triassic Meat-eaters

The first dinosaurs evolved from meat-eating reptiles. Some of the earliest dinosaurs we know of—from as long as 225 million years ago—were also meat-eaters. Lizard-hipped, meat-eating dinosaurs are called theropods (THAIR-uh-podz).

Three-foot-long *Eoraptor* (EE-oh-RAP-tur), a very early dinosaur found in present-day Argentina, had many features that differed from later dinosaurs. Even its teeth were unusual: Some look like a carnivore's, while others look more like a plant-eater's.

Eoraptor

Nine-foot-long *Coelophysis* was not an ordinary meat-eater—it ate its own kind as well as other prey! Scientists found hundreds of *Coelophysis* skeletons at a site in New Mexico. Some, like this one, had small *Coelophysis* bones inside, showing that adults sometimes ate younger ones.

Staurikosaurus (STAW-ri-kuh-SORE-us) is one of the earliest dinosaurs known. This slim, seven-foot-long dinosaur ran on two legs. *Staurikosaurus* skeletons have been found in South America. Their sharp teeth and claws tell us that they ate meat.

Staurikosaurus

The name *Saltopus* (SAWL-toh-pus) means "leaping foot," but this animal used its long hind legs to run, not leap. About the size of a cat, *Saltopus* was fast, which helped it catch and devour prey. So did its long neck, clawed fingers, and sharp teeth. Was *Saltopus* a dinosaur? For a while, experts said yes; now, most say no, but it is a close relative.

Syntarsus (sin-TAR-sus) was a Late Triassic theropod. It got its name, which means "fused ankle," because some of its ankle bones had grown together. Only two feet tall, *Syntarsus* had to avoid being eaten by larger theropods while it searched for smaller prey.

29

Flying Reptiles

Rhamphorhynchus

The first pterosaurs (TER-uh-sores)—flying reptiles—appeared in the Triassic. The last ones vanished at the end of the Cretaceous. Pterosaurs are not dinosaurs, but they took to the skies during dinosaur times.

There were two kinds of pterosaurs. Those like *Rhamphorhynchus* (RAM-fohr-ING-kus) were quite small and had long tails. The other group included *Pterodactylus* (TARE-oh-DAK-til-us) and had longer necks and shorter tails than the first group.

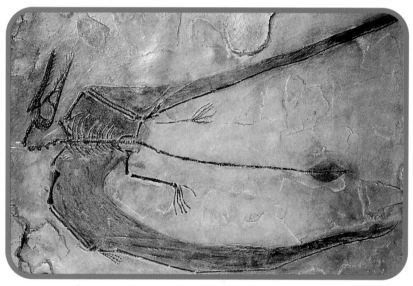

Fossil of a Jurassic *Rhamphorhynchus*

Rhamphorhynchus ate fish. We know this because some *Rhamphorhynchus* fossils have fish bones in their stomachs. This reptile was 18 inches long, with a short neck, a long tail, and a wide wingspan. Its long, pointed jaws were filled with sharp teeth that angled outward. *Rhamphorhynchus* probably flew over the water, snatching up fish near the surface.

30

Quetzalcoatlus (KET-sol-koh-AT-lus) was one of the biggest flying creatures of all time. It cruised over Late Cretaceous Texas on thin wings that may have stretched nearly 40 feet wide (wider than a modern biplane's). Some scientists think that it may have lived much as modern vultures do.

The body of a *Pteranodon* (terr-AN-oh-dahn) was only about the size of a turkey's, but its head—counting the long crest—was 6 feet long! It had a huge wingspan, too: nearly 30 feet wide.

Pteranodon

Life in the Jurassic

Jurassic
sea scene

During the Jurassic Period, Pangaea began to break up (see map, far right). The Atlantic Ocean formed as Africa and the Americas split apart. India started its drift toward Asia. Seas cut into land, bringing rain and helping plants grow in once-dry areas. Jurassic skies were dominated by flying reptiles (*see pp. 30-31*), the seas by marine reptiles. Dinosaurs dominated the land.

Plesiosaurs (PLEE-zee-oh-sores) were not dinosaurs. These Mesozoic creatures, which grew from 8 to 40 feet long, were among the largest marine reptiles. They used their powerful paddle-limbs to "fly" through the water after fish and squid, much as sea turtles do today.

Fossil of a Jurassic Period shrimp

Plesiosaurus

Ichthyosaurs were marine reptiles that appeared during the Triassic and lived through the Jurassic and into the Cretaceous. The ichthyosaur *Ophthalmosaurus* (ahf-THAL-muh-SORE-us), below, had large eyes. (*Ophthalmo-* means "eye" or "eyeball.") These may have helped it hunt for food in the darkness of deep waters.

Ophthalmosaurus

33

Jurassic land scene

During the Jurassic, conifers (trees in the same family as today's redwoods and pines), palmlike cycads (SYE-kadz), and ginkgo trees grew in forests. Dinosaurs dominated, but small mammals and other creatures also roamed the land.

Plant-eating dinosaurs and meat-eating dinosaurs shared the same land areas. Large meat-eaters hunted smaller prey, some of which traveled in groups for protection. Above, a lone meat-eating *Dilophosaurus* (die-LOH-fuh-SORE-us) has its eye on a herd of plant-eating *Anchisaurus* (ANG-kee-SORE-us).

At left: A meat-eating dinosaur is attacking a terrified *Heterodonto-saurus* (HET-ur-uh-DON-toh-SORE-us), which may have eaten plants or animals or both.

Jurassic Plant-eaters

Jurassic plant-eaters included some of the biggest animals ever to walk on Earth. Some were three times as tall as a giraffe and as long as one-and-a-half blue whales! Lizard-hipped, plant-eating dinosaurs are called sauropods (SORE-uh-podz).

Seismosaurus from the side, front, and back.

No one has found a complete *Seismosaurus* (SIZE-muh-SORE-us) yet. Based on bones found so far, though, scientists think that it was 130 to 170 feet long. (That's about half the length of a football field!) Most of its length was in its neck and tail. Like other sauropods, *Seismosaurus* seems to have swallowed stones to help grind up food in its stomach.

Brachiosaurus (BRAK-ee-uh-SORE-us) may have weighed as much as 12 elephants, and was more than 70 feet long and 40 feet high. (It would have had no problem peeking over the top of a four-story building!) Its bones have been found in western North America and in East Africa.

Seismosaurus from above.

36

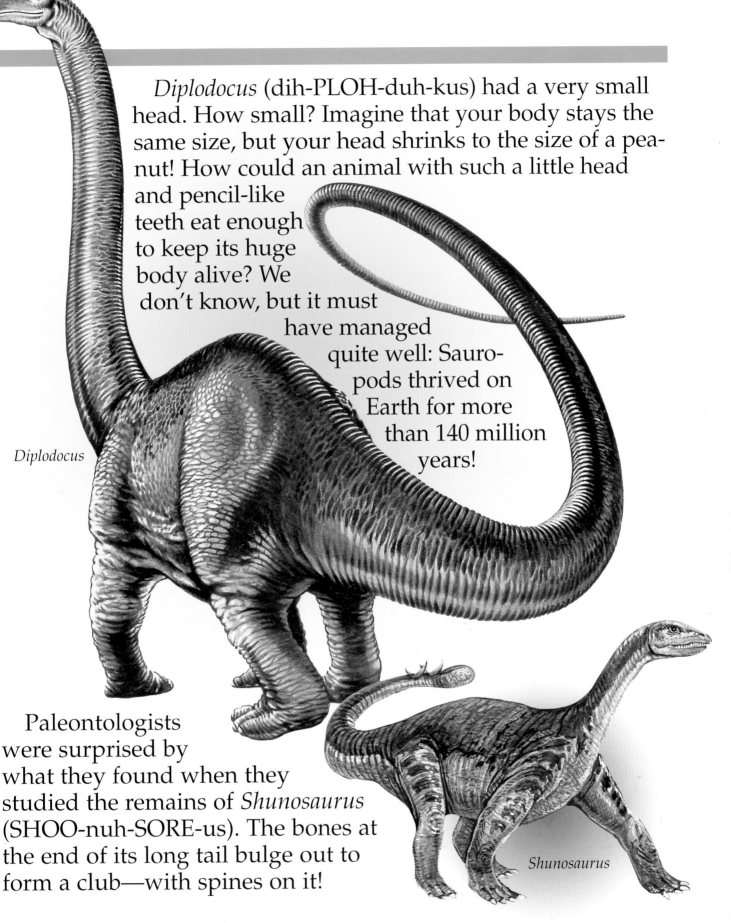

Diplodocus (dih-PLOH-duh-kus) had a very small head. How small? Imagine that your body stays the same size, but your head shrinks to the size of a peanut! How could an animal with such a little head and pencil-like teeth eat enough to keep its huge body alive? We don't know, but it must have managed quite well: Sauropods thrived on Earth for more than 140 million years!

Diplodocus

Paleontologists were surprised by what they found when they studied the remains of *Shunosaurus* (SHOO-nuh-SORE-us). The bones at the end of its long tail bulge out to form a club—with spines on it!

Shunosaurus

Mamenchisaurus (mah-MEN-chih-SORE-us) was 70 feet long—and half of that was its neck! That puts it in the record books as having the longest neck of any animal ever known. Its name comes from where it was found: Mamenchi, China.

Besides the great sauropods, other plant-eating dinosaurs grazed their way through the Jurassic.

Most dinosaurs had only one kind of teeth: either the kind that grind up plants or the kind that tear into flesh. *Heterodontosaurus* had three kinds (as do humans): sharp teeth in the front, longer teeth (fangs) on each side, and wider teeth in back. It was among the first dinosaurs to have cheeks—a place to hold food while chewing.

Heterodontosaurus head (above) and skull (below).

Camptosaurus

Several different species of *Camptosaurus* (KAMP-tuh-SORE-us) lived in North America and Europe near the end of the Jurassic. This 20-foot-long ornithischian (bird-hipped dinosaur) probably walked on its hind legs most of the time, but sometimes walked on all four.

Anchisaurus

Some prosauropods—the earliest-known plant-eating dinosaurs—were still around during the Jurassic Period. Some were large, like 30-foot-long *Riojasaurus* (ree-OH-hah-SORE-us). Others, such as *Anchisaurus* (ANG-kee-SORE-us), never reached 10 feet.

Riojasaurus

Jurassic Stegosaurs

Stegosaurs (STEG-uh-sores) were dinosaurs whose bodies had an armor made of plates, spikes, or both. Clearly, these Jurassic plant-eaters did *not* want to become a meat-eater's next meal!

The single row of plates along the back of 25-foot-long *Stegosaurus* (STEG-uh-SORE-us) may have helped the animal control its body temperature by soaking up the sun to warm its body or releasing heat to cool it. *Stegosaurus* had four heavy spikes, nearly four feet long, at the end of its tail.

Left: A herd of armor-plated *Scutellosaurus* fleeing from a *Dilophosaurus*.

More than 300 armor plates were found with the skeleton of a *Scutellosaurus* (skoo-TELL-uh-SORE-us). The living animal may have had more.

DID YOU KNOW . . . ?
Even the biggest stegosaurs had brains that were no larger than a dog's.

Kentrosaurus

Kentrosaurus (KEN-truh-SORE-us) had plates about half-way down its back. From there to the tip of its tail, this 15-foot-long plant-eater had pairs of spikes! It also had a pair of spikes coming out from its shoulders. The spikes probably served *Kentrosaurus* as a defense against predators.

Jurassic Meat-eaters

Jurassic theropods (meat-eating dinosaurs that walked on their hind legs) came in both large and small sizes.

Dilophosaurus
on the prowl

With twin crests decorating the top of its head, *Dilophosaurus* (dye-LOH-fuh-SORE-us) certainly stood out. About 20 feet long, it had long, slender teeth and a lightly built skull. This makes scientists think that it may have been more of a scavenger than an active hunter. (A scavenger eats already-dead or injured animals, rather than killing them itself.)

Dilophosaurus skull

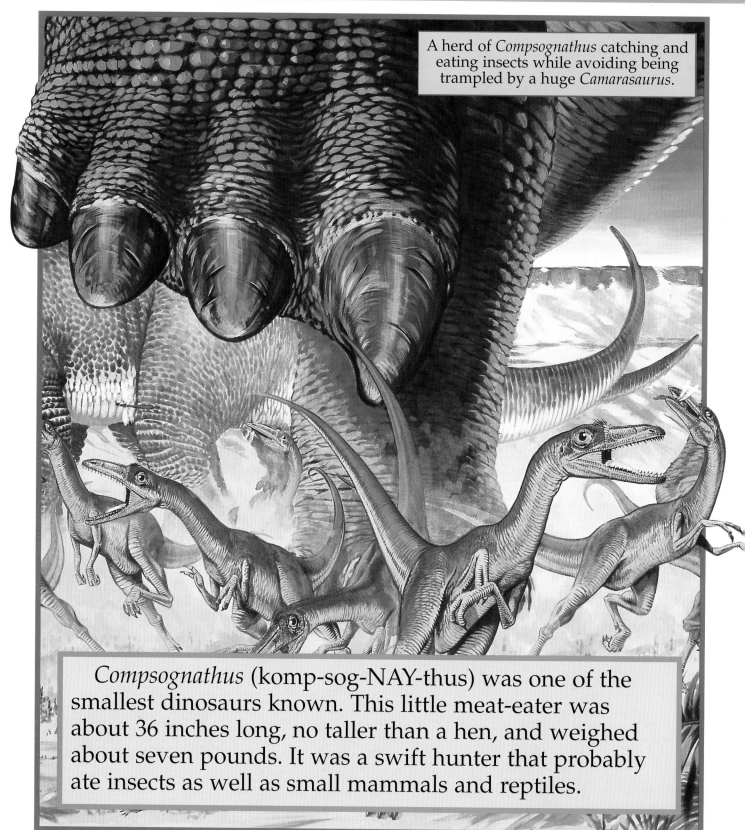

A herd of *Compsognathus* catching and eating insects while avoiding being trampled by a huge *Camarasaurus*.

Compsognathus (komp-sog-NAY-thus) was one of the smallest dinosaurs known. This little meat-eater was about 36 inches long, no taller than a hen, and weighed about seven pounds. It was a swift hunter that probably ate insects as well as small mammals and reptiles.

Megalosaurus was not the first dinosaur whose bones were found (that was *Iguanodon*), but it was the first to be named. Its name, which means "big lizard," really fits: *Megalosaurus* was 30 feet long and, when standing, 12 feet tall! Like all theropods, its long tail probably helped it keep its balance.

Allosaurus attacking a young *Diplodocus*.

With its light skeleton and long legs, *Ornitholestes* (OR-nih-thuh-LES-teez) must have been a very quick runner. The name *Ornitholestes* means "bird robber," but it probably ate small reptiles, mammals, and frogs—and other dinosaurs.

Allosaurus (AL-uh-SORE-us), which was 30 to 40 feet long, had big, strong hind legs that may have allowed it to run almost 20 miles an hour. Its head, alone, was as big as an entire *Comp-sognathus*! Its jaws were packed with more than 73 teeth, each tooth an inch long.

A Rustle of Feathers

When did the first bird appear? Are birds descendants of the dinosaurs? Paleontologists look for clues in rocks from the Jurassic and Cretaceous periods. Fossils of flying animals are rare. Most flew over land, so when they died, their bodies were probably eaten by other animals before they could be preserved. Their light bones, which helped them fly, would have broken easily.

Sinosauropteryx

Caudipteryx

Caudipteryx (kaw-DIP-ter-iks), a feathered dinosaur, seems to be on the border between non-avian (not a bird) dinosaurs and birds. About three feet long, it was a swift runner that didn't have the right kind of feathers to fly.

Sinosauropteryx (SYE-noh-sore-OP-ter-iks), found in China, is like a chicken-sized, meat-eating dinosaur. It is clearly not a bird, but its fossils have something different from those of most other dinosaurs: things that look like feathers! It may have been an ancestor of today's birds.

46

This fossil, found in Germany, is one of the most famous in the world. It is *Archaeopteryx* (AR-kee-OP-ter-iks), which lived 150 million years ago. This small, meat-eating dinosaur with feathers is the earliest-known bird. The shape of its feathers suggests that it flew instead of just gliding, but probably not far.

DID YOU KNOW . . . ?
Most experts say that dinosaurs are not extinct! They remain on Earth—in the form of their descendants, birds.

Some well-preserved fossils were found in China recently. Several are of an early bird called *Confuciusornis* (kon-FYOO-shuh-SORE-nis). Unlike *Archaeopteryx*, which had a mouth full of teeth, *Confuciusornis* had a toothless beak similar to that of modern birds. It is the earliest-known bird that was able to fly for any distance.

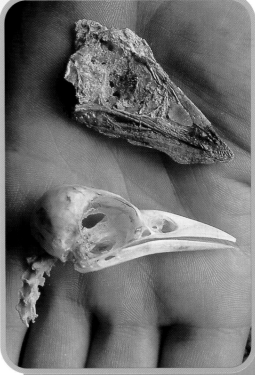

Top: *Confuciusornis*, 120 million years old. Bottom: Old World oriole, a modern-day bird.

Life in the Cretaceous

It was a wet world during the Cretaceous Period. The seas rose more than 600 feet higher than today's level. That covered almost half of what is now dry land. In North America, an inland sea grew and shrank several times. Mountains rose and volcanoes erupted along the west coast of the Americas. The climate was warmer then: There was no ice to be found—not even at the poles!

This painting shows some of the dinosaurs that lived during the Cretaceous—at various times and in various parts of the world.

The marine lizard above, *Tylosaurus* (TY-loh-SORE-us), was not a dinosaur. It swam in the sea that stretched across North America, from the Arctic Ocean to the Gulf of Mexico, during the Late Cretaceous. *Tylosaurus* grew up to 40 feet long. Its limbs were more like flippers than arms and legs. It used its gigantic jaws and sharp teeth to snap up fish and other sea animals.

North America
Niobrara
Sea
Europe &
Asia
South
America
Africa
India
Antarctica
Australia

**DID
YOU KNOW . . . ?**
The first flowering plants
appeared during the
Cretaceous Period. This
made a big change in
how the world
looked!

Duckbills

One group of Cretaceous plant-eating dinosaurs was called hadrosaurs (HAD-ruh-sores). They had long, wide snouts ending in broad beaks that looked something like a duck's bill. From that came their nickname: the duckbilled dinosaurs.

Duckbills' teeth were crammed into their jaws in stacks of three to five replacement teeth under each working tooth. Up to 60 stacks and 1,200 teeth were packed into a single duckbill mouth!

A duckbill skull

From a distant shore, a hunting *Tyrannosaurus* eyes herds of various kinds of duckbilled dinosaurs.

There were two kinds of duckbills. Those like *Anatosaurus* (ah-NAT-uh-SORE-us), at right, had a flat head without a bony crest. The other group, which included *Lambeosaurus* (LAM-bee-uh-SORE-us), below, had fancy, hollow crests.

Shantungosaurus (SHAN-tung-uh-SORE-us), above, lived in China. The biggest of all duckbills, it was about 50 feet long and weighed around 9 tons.

The name *Maiasaura* (MY-uh-SORE-uh) means "good mother lizard." Paleontologist John Horner named this duckbilled dinosaur after he found fossils, in Montana in 1979, suggesting that it took care of its babies. Until *Maiasaura* was found, scientists thought that dinosaurs just laid their eggs and left the babies to take care of themselves after they hatched, as most reptiles do.

Each *Maiasaura* mother shaped her seven-foot-wide nest out of dirt and laid her eggs. Then she covered them with grass and dirt, to help keep them warm. Maiasaur parents apparently took food back to the nest for their young. Adults probably spit up food that they had already chewed and partially digested. This would be easier for the babies to eat.

Iguanodon

Iguanodon (ih-GWAHN-uh-don) was a plant-eating dinosaur of the Early Cretaceous. It was only the second dinosaur ever described. British amateur paleontologist Gideon Mantell studied fossil teeth found in a gravel pit. He guessed right when he said that they were for chewing plants. Since the teeth looked like an iguana's, he decided that they must have come from a huge, iguanalike animal.

Iguanodon under attack by small theropods.

DID YOU KNOW . . . ?

Iguanodon had no front teeth, but its back teeth were wide and flat. Today's herbivores use teeth like that for grinding the plants they eat. At the front of *Iguanodon*'s jaws was a horny, self-sharpening beak much like that of a tortoise. This worked well for chopping twigs and leaves.

Iguanodon was about 30 feet long, with a long, heavy tail that probably helped it keep its balance—whether it walked on its back legs, as young ones did, or on all fours, as larger, heavier ones did. *Iguanodon* tracks have been found in rocks throughout Europe.

Iguanodon's bony thumbs

Early drawings of *Iguanodon* show it with a spiky horn on its nose. That "horn" was really a pointed, bony thumb (above). But no one realized that until a skeleton was found with the bone in the right place.

In 1878, 24 nearly complete *Iguanodon* skeletons were found in a Belgian coal mine. The skeletons helped give scientists a much better idea of what *Iguanodon* looked like.

More Cretaceous Plant-eaters

Ten-foot-long *Dravidosaurus* (druh-VID-uh-SORE-us) is the only stegosaur known from near the end of dinosaur times.

Cretaceous herbivores (plant-eaters) came in assorted sizes.

Hypsilopho-don (HIP-suh-LOH-fuh-don), below, was only about seven-and-a-half feet long. Walking with its tail up and head forward, it would have been about two feet off the ground at its hips.

Alamosaurus (AL-uh-moh-SORE-us)— one of the biggest Cretaceous plant-eaters—was nearly 70 feet long.

Ouranosaurus (oo-RAN-oh-SORE-us) was about 24 feet long and had long spines on its back-bone. It may have had a sail like *Spinosaurus* (SPY-nuh-SORE-us), a meat-eating dinosaur that lived about the same time and place.

Stegoceras (steg-OH-ser-us) was one of the dinosaurs nicknamed "bone-heads." Its dome-shaped skull had a roof of bone three inches thick, with a spiky frill. What was it for? Experts used to think that *Stegoceras* males butted heads, as bighorn sheep do today, but no one really knows.

Above: An *Alamosaurus* trio defends itself from an *Albertosaurus* attack.

57

Plant-eaters in Armor

Some Cretaceous plant-eaters relied on armor to keep them from becoming another dinosaur's lunch. Armored dinosaurs belong to a family called Ankylosauria (an-KYE-low-SORE-ee-ah). That name means "fused lizards."

Edmontonia (ED-mon-TOH-nee-uh) was the largest of the nodosaurs. It grew to a length of about 25 feet. Predators had to beware of those spikes coming from its sides!

Two types of dinosaurs belonged to the Ankylosauria group: ankylosaurs and nodosaurs (NOH-doh-sores). Both had bony plates called scutes (SKOOTS) protecting their bodies. Ankylosaurs had wide heads and clubs at the end of their tails. Nodosaurs had narrow heads, sideways-pointing spikes, and tails without clubs.

The smallest known member of Ankylosauria was *Struthiosaurus* (STROO-thee-oh-SORE-us), a six-foot-long nodosaur.

58

Minmi (MIN-my) was a nodosaur. A blanket of very small scutes protected its tender stomach. *Minmi* is the dinosaur with the shortest name! (It was named for a rock formation in Australia, where it was found.)

Euoplocephalus (yoo-OP-luh-SEF-uh-lus) was an ankylosaur—look at that tail! It had spikes, and was armored from head to tail. It even had armored eyelids that could be shut like window shades to protect its eyes.

59

Plant-eaters With Horns

One group of Cretaceous plant-eating dinosaurs is called ceratopians (SER-uh-TOP-ee-uns). That means "horned faces"—and you can see why! These rhinoceroslike animals had a wide assortment of bony horns and neck frills.

Right: *Styracosaurus* (sty-RAK-uh-SORE-us), seemed to have horns and spikes sticking out all over its head. The spikes on its frill probably were used for display.

Triceratops (try-SER-uh-tops) was 25 feet long and weighed more than an elephant. Its skull alone was over six feet long!

60

Torosaurus had a huge head. One skeleton was found with a head 8.5 feet long—the second-biggest head of any land animal ever known! The frill of a *Torosaurus* was even longer than its head.

Left: This *Triceratops* herd is circling to protect its young while using its horns to defend itself from a *Tyrannosaurus* attack.

Not all ceratopians were large. *Microceratops* (MYE-kroh-SER-uh-tops) was one of the smallest of all dinosaurs: only 30 inches long! The group of *Microceratops* below is hiding from a *Tarbosaurus*.

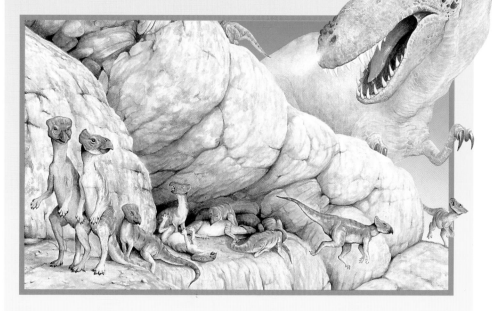

Cretaceous Hunters

Cretaceous meat-eating dinosaurs came in all shapes and sizes.

A *Baryonyx* claw fossil

Talons nearly one foot long earned *Baryonyx* (BAYR-ee-ON-iks) the nickname "Claws." This 30-foot-long, Early Cretaceous dinosaur was expert at catching fish, its favorite food. It had a long snout filled with teeth, something like a crocodile's. *Baryonyx* had twice as many teeth as other meat-eaters!

62

One of the largest meat-eaters ever, 40-foot-long *Spinosaurus* had spines up to 6.5 feet long coming out of its backbone. What was that "sail" for? The extra skin surface may have helped cold-blooded *Spinosaurus* get more heat from the sun when it was cold, and cool down its huge body when it was hot.

Acrocanthosaurus (AK-roh-KAN-thuh-SORE-us) had foot-long spines on its neck, back, and tail. Unlike *Spinosaurus*'s thin sail, these spines were covered in a thick ridge of flesh. Strong muscles attached to the spines gave *Acrocanthosaurus* great power for catching and tearing apart prey.

Dromaeosaurus (DROH-mee-uh-SORE-us) had a large brain and big eyes in its birdlike head. Just six feet long, it was probably a smart, quick hunter that grabbed small prey, then ripped into it with a special toe claw.

Below: Little *Dromaeosaurus* feeding on prey killed by a larger hunter.

Utahraptor (YOO-tah-RAP-tor), at right, was a larger relative of *Dromaeosaurus*. It has been called one of the most intelligent—and vicious—of all dinosaurs. Its toe claw may have been more than 15 inches long.

Utahraptor

A movie-model version of *Velociraptor*

Velociraptor is a well-named dinosaur. This man-sized hunter's name means "swift thief," and it was built for speed, with a light-boned body and long, sturdy legs. It was also built for catching and killing prey: Its hands and feet ended in big, sharp claws.

Oviraptor (OH-vee-RAP-tor) means "egg thief," because the first *Oviraptor* fossil found (in the 1920s) was on top of eggs thought to belong to *Protoceratops*. But in 1993, an *Oviraptor* embryo was found inside an egg of the same type! The fossil above is of a mother *Oviraptor* with her own eggs.

65

Ostrich-mimics

A group of ostrichlike dinosaurs lived during the Later Cretaceous. They ran swiftly on long, thin hind legs. They probably ate small reptiles, mammals, and insects. Scientists think that they may also have eaten the eggs of other animals.

WORDS FOR THE WISE

The scientific name for this group of dinosaurs is ornithomimids (OR-nith-oh-MYE-midz). It comes from two Greek words that perfectly describe what they are: *ornith*, meaning "bird," and *mimos*, meaning "imitator"!

At left: *Gallimimus* (GAL-ih-MYE-mus), 13 feet long, was the biggest ostrich-mimic dinosaur.

66

Dromiceiomimus

Twelve-foot-long *Dromiceio-mimus* (DROH-mee-see-uh-MYE-mus) may have been one of the fastest dinosaurs. It may have been able to run up to 40 miles an hour! It could use that speed in two ways: to catch up to prey, and to escape from larger predators.

Below: *Struthiomimus*

Struthiomimus (STROO-thee-uh-MYE-mus) was 10 to 13 feet long and 8 feet tall. Its long, strong hands ended in three claw-tipped fingers. It wasn't the fastest ornith-omimid but, even at half speed, it could have kept pace with a world-class human athlete in a 100-meter race!

Troodon

Troodon (TROH-oh-don)—a human-sized, meat-eating dinosaur—had a lot of brain for its body size. It was one of the smartest of all dinosaurs.

Troodon skull

Troodon's sharp teeth, long claws, and other features mark it as a swift-running hunter and meat-eater.

With its long, slim tail to help balance its long, thin legs, *Troodon* was probably very speedy—and good at making quick turns. The long fingers on its hands would have been good for snatching up small reptiles and mammals.

Each of *Troodon's* eyes was almost two inches wide. Such big eyes may mean that it hunted in low light, at dusk or nighttime.

Troodon had many sharp teeth, hence its name: *troo* is Greek for "to wound"; *don,* for "tooth."

Deinonychus

Scientists used to think that meat-eating dinosaurs were slow-moving animals. But in 1964, *Deinonychus* (dye-NON-ih-kus) was discovered—and made scientists rethink their ideas.

Deinonychus had long, strong arms ending in three-fingered hands with sharp claws. It could grab and hold on to prey.

On the second toe of each foot, *Deinonychus* had a curved claw that was up to five inches long. The dino-saur may have balanced on one foot and kicked at prey with the other, using the claw to make deep wounds. The claws stayed sharp because they were held off the ground when *Deinonychus* walked or ran.

70

Hunting alone, *Deinonychus* probably ate small reptiles and mammals. There is some evidence that it hunted in packs; if two or three teamed up, they could have handled larger prey with ease.

DID YOU KNOW . . . ? The name *Deinonychus* means "terrible claw."

Deinonychus was 10 feet long, but light for its size. (It probably weighed about the same as an adult human.) Its tail, stiffened by bony tendons, stuck nearly straight out. This helped *Deinonychus* balance as it jumped and ran.

Tyrannosaurus & Company

Was *Tyrannosaurus* an active hunter or did it just look for dead animals to eat? Like many of today's meat-eaters, it probably did both.

Tyrannosaurus (tye-RAN-uh-SORE-us) may be the most famous dinosaur of all. At 40 to 50 feet long, this giant was one of the biggest meat-eaters to ever walk on Earth.

Old models of *Tyrannosaurus* show it standing up with its tail on the ground. Today, we know that it leaned forward with its tail up and out, to balance its large, heavy head.

The head of a *Tyrannosaurus* was more than 4.5 feet long!

DID YOU KNOW . . . ?
Tyrannosaurus belongs to a group of dinosaurs, called tyrannosaurids (tye-RAN-uh-SAW-ridz), that looked a lot like it. (Turn the page to see some of its relatives.)

Tyrannosaurus teeth (below left, and at right) were one inch wide and up to six inches long. They were shaped and serrated like steak knives, to cut through flesh and bone. Scientists think that *Tyrannosaurus* could rip off a 500-pound chunk of meat with just one bite of its powerful jaws!

73

There is no doubt that *Carcharodontosaurus* (kar-KAR-oh-DON-tuh-SORE-us) was a mighty meat-eater. Look at all these huge, sharp teeth! That long name is a perfect fit: It comes from the Greek words for "sharp" (*karcharo*), "teeth" (*odontos*), and "lizard" (*sauros*).

DID YOU KNOW...? Tyranno-saurids were around for only about the last 15 million years of dinosaur time. We know of only a few dinosaurs of this type.

At 26 feet in length, *Albertosaurus* (al-BUR-tuh-SORE-us) was big, but only about half the size of its huge relative, *Tyrannosaurus*. Though smaller, it was just as fierce a hunter. *Albertosaurus* lived at the end of the Cretaceous Period.

Two tyrannosaurids compete for food in this scene of life in the Late Cretaceous Period.

End of the Dinosaurs?

Most dinosaurs vanished at the end of the Cretaceous. Scientists are still trying to figure out why and how. No one idea seems to explain the whole story.

DON'T FORGET!
Some experts say that dinosaurs remain on Earth in the form of their descendants, birds.

One theory is that an asteroid (a rock from space) crashed into Earth. This could have changed the environment, making it harmful to most dinosaurs. Some scientists think that the extinction occurred all at once. Others think that dinosaurs were already in trouble—the asteroid just finished them off.

Dinosaurs were not the only type of life to face extinction around the end of the Cretaceous Period. Many other kinds of animals also disappeared then, too, including flying reptiles, some kinds of mammals, and many marine animals. Many kinds of plants also died out.

The great seas were shrinking at the end of the Cretaceous. This may have let migrating dinosaurs mix with each other for the first time. Diseases or new predators may have killed off many dinosaurs. Other ideas about why most dinosaurs disappeared include new poisonous plants and mammals eating dinosaur eggs.

What Came Next

About 16 million years ago, the giant shark *Carcharodon megalodon* (kar-KAR-uh-don MEG-uh-la-don) began to hunt the seas. Scientists think that it was 40 to 45 feet long—about four times the length of today's fierce predator, the great white shark.

Teeth from a shark of 10 million years ago (left) and a great white shark of today.

With the majority of dinosaurs gone (birds remained), other kinds of animals moved into areas that dinosaurs had dominated. Many different kinds of plants and animals evolved. Mammals—relatively minor in dinosaur days—became the dominant type of animal life on Earth.

The Cenozoic Era (mya = million years ago)

Paleocene Epoch	Eocene Epoch	Oligocene Epoch	Miocene Epoch	Pliocene Epoch	Pleistocene Epoch	Holocene Epoch
65 to 57 mya	57 to 35 mya	35 to 25 mya	23 to 5 mya	5 to 1.65 mya	1.65 million to 10,000 years ago	10,000 years ago to today

The first horse, *Hyracotherium* (HYE-rak-uh-THAIR-ee-um), was only about a foot tall. It evolved around the same time grasses did, but did not eat them—its teeth were not suited for grazing. Its descendants, however, became grazers.

Above: *Hyracotherium*

About 2 million years ago, a Great Ice Age began. Then, about 10,000 years ago, things began to warm up again. The climate changes were hard on animal life, and many species became extinct.

This painting shows a scene of plant and animal life in Europe during the Tertiary Period (65-1.65 mya). After the first grasses appeared, about 50 million years ago, so did deer and other animals that lived by eating grass.

Strangers Passing Through

In the 65 million years since most dinosaurs became extinct, some weird and wonderful animals appeared—then disappeared. Imagine: What might our world be like if they were still around?

Some mammals that lived during the Miocene Epoch (23 to 5 million years ago).

Bigger than a car, the giant *Glyptodon* (GLIP-tuh-don) lived about two million years ago. This armadillolike mammal had a bony "helmet" growing on its head and a tough shell covering its back, sides, and tail.

Brontotherium was a relative of the modern-day rhinoceros. This big plant-eater lived about 30 million years ago. Its ancestors were animals about the size of a dog, and had no horns, but they evolved into the rhino-sized animal above. No one knows how *Brontotherium* used its slingshot-shaped horns.

The woolly mammoth looked a lot like a very hairy elephant with giant tusks. It disappeared about 10,000 years ago.

Phorusrhacus (FOR-rus-RAY-kus), a big, ostrichlike bird, grew to a height of about five feet. This meat-eater had the right tools for hunting: a sharp, hook-shaped beak and sharp talons. It lived about 20 million years ago on the plains of South America.

About two million years ago, one of the main predators was *Smilodon* (SMYE-luh-don), a big, saber-toothed catlike animal.

Still Around

Whatever killed off most dinosaurs at the end of the Cretaceous Period did not harm everything. Some plants and animals from before, during, and soon after the Mesozoic Era, when dinosaurs dominated Earth, are still around today.

Sharks appeared nearly 400 million years ago, looking very much the same as now.

Turtles have not changed much over time. Compare this tortoise of today with a fossil that is 35 million years old.

Today's crocodile (top) and the Triassic's *Euparkeria*

Modern-day crocodiles can trace their ancestry back to early dinosaur times. *Euparkeria*, a Triassic reptile, was closely related to the ancestor of dinosaurs—and probably to crocodiles as well.

Left: A fossil coelacanth from the Jurassic Period. Below: Model of a coelacanth caught in 1938.

Scientists once thought that the coelacanth (SEE-luh-kanth), a fish that was around before the dinosaurs, became extinct 75 million years ago. Then, in 1938, a living coelacanth was found near the Comoros Islands of Africa! A few still remain, almost unchanged from prehistoric times.

Dragonflies living today look a lot like those living 250 million years ago. (Compare this one of today with the one on page 19.) There is one big difference, however: Today's dragonfly has a wingspan of about 7.5 inches. Back then, some were as wide as 2.5 feet!

Horseshoe crabs (left) look the same today as they did about 300 million years ago.

Lampreys are a kind of fish that showed up before the dinosaurs, looking almost the same as they do today.

The oldest vulture fossils come from the Eocene Epoch (57 to 35 mya). Like modern-day vultures, they were raptors (birds of prey). While many raptors hunt and kill for their food, vultures prefer to feed on already-dead animals.

This lappet-face vulture looks and lives much the same way vultures did 50 million years ago.

Many plants from prehistoric times are still around, including ginkgo trees, monkey-puzzle trees, giant redwoods, and cycads (SYE-kadz). The fossil cycad above (a palmlike tropical plant) is from the Jurassic Period.

In the Field

When paleontologists look for dinosaur fossils, they start by finding rocks of a certain age and type. Then they look for pieces of bone sticking out of the rock or lying on the ground. Old bones look a lot like rock, but sometimes you can tell them apart by licking them: Bone sticks to your tongue, rock doesn't!

After mapping the site, the next step is to remove dirt and excess stone. Paleontologists use different tools to do this, from dynamite to jackhammers to drills to the most delicate chisels and brushes.

Before moving anything from its original site, experts often map out the site in a grid pattern, like the one above. Then they make careful drawings of everything in its place, showing its relative size and position to its surroundings. Electronic measuring equipment can be used to put the same information directly into a computer.

Once a specimen has been completely uncovered, experts seal it in a protective coating of plaster—the same stuff used to make casts to protect broken human bones.

With one specimen safely in its plaster jacket, this paleontologist is working to uncover the next section of a dinosaur skeleton. Once the specimens are ready, they will be transported to a lab.

In the Lab

When a fossil arrives at the lab, the careful work of removing it from the rock begins. The lab is where paleontologists finally get to see what they have found. New technologies help them learn more from the fossils.

Some fossils, such as the dinosaur egg at left, are too rare or fragile to risk cutting them open to see what is inside. A CAT scan, which doctors use to look inside people's bodies, shows the insides of a fossil without damaging it. A CAT scan can show the bones of a baby dinosaur curled up in an egg!

A preparator (pruh-PAIR-uh-tor) carefully removes all the wrappings from the fossil. Then he or she slowly chips the rock away from the bone, often using tools like those your dentist uses to clean teeth. Sometimes the preparator puts the fossil under a microscope and uses a very fine needle. The cleaned fossil is coated with a clear glue to protect it.

This fossil was an oreodont, an Oligocene Epoch mammal.

DID YOU KNOW . . . ?

Some scientists use computer programs that "morph" fossils to show, step by step, how one object might have developed into another. This helps give us an idea of what an extinct animal looked like as it grew from baby to adult.

Clearing, cleaning, and sealing a fossil must be done very slowly and carefully. It takes a long time! That is why many fossils found and sent to labs are still in storage, still in their field wrappings, waiting to be cleaned.

Some Things We've Found

We usually think of fossils as bones, but they can also be things like teeth, wood, shell, footprints, or impressions left by bits of skin or fur. Fossils come in all shapes, sizes, and kinds. Paleontologists study—and learn from—them all.

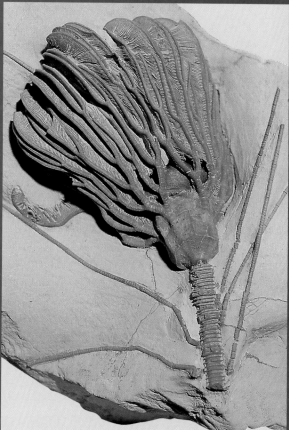

Some fossils are only a few bones, but sometimes a nearly complete specimen is found. The Jurassic *Compsognathus* above, found in southern Germany, had very few parts missing.

This weird-looking fossil may look like a plant, but it was a sea animal called a crinoid (KRY-noyd). (This one lived way before dinosaurs, back in the Devonian Period.) It was a member of the echinoderm family—the same family as today's starfish and sea urchins.

Herring fossil

Who ate what way back when? Fossils that capture animals in the midst of everyday acts provide experts with valuable information about how those animals lived. The fish above—a herring—was trapped in the act of eating another, smaller fish of its own kind.

Scientists even study the stuff dinosaurs no longer had any use for—coprolites, for instance. Coprolites are fossilized dinosaur droppings (feces). They come in different shapes and sizes, depending on the dinosaur that left them—and what it ate.

Amber fossils are among the most beautiful. Amber is fossilized resin, a substance that oozes out of trees—and sometimes traps animals inside before it hardens. This piece of amber has held a spider, along with several small insects, for almost 30 million years.

93

Worldwide Fossil Finds

▲ **Triassic**

● **Jurassic**

■ **Cretaceous**

North America

South America

Antarctica

Dinosaur fossils have been found on every continent, including Antarctica. This map shows some sites of major dinosaur-fossil finds. (To find out what the world looked like when these animals lived, compare this map with the maps at the top of pages 23, 33, and 49.) New discoveries are made all the time, forcing experts to rethink long-held ideas about dinosaurs.

Interpreting Data:
Bringing Bones to Life

What did now-extinct dinosaurs look like? Paleontologists start with information gained from studying skeletons, teeth, and other fossils. Then they consult with experts who know about animal muscles, eyes, skin, and many other details. That helps them come up with a picture of something that no human has ever seen!

Teeth give important clues about what an animal ate and how it lived. Plant-eaters like *Corythosaurus* (skull above) had relatively short, blunt teeth. Meat-eaters had longer, thinner, and sharper teeth, like those of *Coelophysis* (skull below).

Scars on bones are a clue to where muscles were attached. By putting bones together and studying their size, shape, and weight, experts can figure out what the muscles attached to those bones probably looked like. This then helps them figure out whether the animal was fast or slow, powerful or weak, bulky or slim.

Paintings like the dramatic scene at right, of a *Barosaurus* being attacked by an *Allosaurus*, don't just spring up in an artist's imagination. The painter had the animals' skeletons to go by (photo, below right), plus information on who ate what, gained from the study of fossils.

Interpreting Data:
Babies

Through studying fossils, paleontologists have learned a great deal about how now-extinct dinosaurs were born.

Were dinosaurs born live or did they hatch from eggs? Finding fossils like the one above—a nest of *Oviraptor* eggs found in China's Gobi Desert—settled that question for at least one dinosaur species.

When a dinosaur nest was found in the 1920s, paleontologists thought that it belonged to *Protoceratops*. They used that and other information to come up with this picture of *Protoceratops* growing from hatchling to adult. It is not completely wrong—*Protoceratops* did hatch from eggs—but the eggs shown belong to *Oviraptor*.

Though experts can find out what is inside a dinosaur egg without cracking it open (*see p. 90*), they also learn from dinosaur embryo skeletons that have been reassembled, such as the Cretaceous duckbill at left.

Sometimes, experts with incomplete fossils build models to show what a complete creature may have looked like. The model at right shows a baby *Maiasaura* hatching from an egg.

Interpreting Data:
Trackways

Did a dinosaur walk upright or on all fours? Was it slow and heavy, or a fast-running lightweight? Experts can find out that and more by studying fossilized footprints called trackways.

The fossilized dinosaur footprint below was found in Page, Arizona.

TRY IT YOURSELF!
To find out how paleontologists "read" trackways, get some friends together and make your own tracks. In soft, muddy ground, try walking, jumping, and running. Then study the tracks. Which tracks came from which activity? How can you tell?

What's in a Name?

Fossil dinosaurs are named after different things—a person, where the bones were found, how the bones look, or how paleontologists think the animal behaved, for example.

The full name of this species of meat-eater, which lived in China during the Jurassic Period, is *Gasosaurus constructus* (GAS-uh-SORE-us kun-STRUK-tus). It was named for gas-company construction workers, who found its bones.

Tyrannosaurus rex is the name of a species, but one *T. rex* fossil—the largest and most complete ever found—has a nickname: Sue. It was named for Sue Hendrickson, the paleontologist who found it in Montana in 1990. In the photo below, she holds one of its bones.

DID YOU KNOW . . . ?

A dinosaur found in China in 1993 owes its name to the popular movie *Jurassic Park*. Its full name is *Tianchisaurus nedegoatpeferima*. The second word was made by taking the first two letters of the surnames of the movie's stars: Sam **NE**ill, Laura **DE**rn, Jeff **GO**ldblum, Richard **AT**tenborough, Bob **PE**ck, Martin **FE**rrero, Ariana **RI**chards, and Joseph **MA**zello.

See Them Yourself!

Now that you've read about these prehistoric animals, you might like to see some for yourself. Dinosaur fossils, models, and exhibits can be found at national parks and monuments as well as natural history museums. Some quarries and other dig sites are open to the public. Go visit an extinct dinosaur today!

Seeing bones up close at Dinosaur National Monument in Colorado/Utah.

This park ranger is showing how experts are digging huge bones out of rock.

Museum exhibits include fossils still in rock, models based on fossils, photographs, paintings—and many other ways you can learn more about dinosaurs.

Many museums have impressive displays of dinosaur skeletons.

Paleontologist Patricia Vickers-Rich prepares a skeleton of *Tarbosaurus bataar*, found in Mongolia, for an exhibit.

Glossary

Amphibians: cold-blooded animals that can live on both land and in water. Unlike reptiles, amphibians do not have scales and they lay their eggs in water. As far as we know, *Mastodonsaurus* was the largest amphibian that ever lived.

Ankylosauria: one of three types of ornithischian dinosaurs, these "armored dinosaurs" ate plants, walked on four legs, and had bony plates and spikes protecting their bodies. There were two types of Ankylosauria dinosaurs: ankylosaurs and nodosaurs.

Ankylosaurs: one of two types of Ankylosauria dinosaurs, ankylosaurs had wide heads and a club on their tails. (Compare with NODOSAURS.)

Archaeology: the scientific study of the fossils, artifacts, and other remains of human life in past ages.

Armor: a skinlike covering made of fused bone plates that protected certain dinosaurs, such as Ankylosauria, from attack.

Carnivore: an animal that eats the flesh of other animals; a meat-eater.

Ceratopians: one of three types of ornithischian dinosaurs, these plant-eating dinosaurs had heavy bodies, walked on all fours, and had a frill or crest on their necks; most had horns on their faces.

Cold-blooded: having a body temperature that is not regulated internally, but adapts to the temperature of surrounding air or water.

Conifer: an evergreen tree or shrub, such as today's redwoods and pines. Some conifers thrived during the Jurassic Period.

Crest: a projection or ridge of bone on the heads of certain dinosaurs.

Epoch: a division of geologic time (such as the Miocene) that is less than a period and greater than an age.

Era: one of the five major divisions of geologic time, such as the Paleozoic.

Evolve: to gradually change or develop.

Extinction: the death of a population of animals caused by predators, a loss of habitat, or the inability to adapt to changes in the environment.

Fossil: the remains or impression of an animal or plant naturally preserved in rock or other hard substances.

Frill: a collar of bone that grew behind the skull of certain dinosaurs. The large frill of *Triceratops* may have protected its neck from attackers.

Herbivore: an animal that eats plants.

Mammals: warm-blooded animals that nourish their young with milk and have skin covered with hair. Humans, apes, dogs, and horses are all mammals.

Migrating: an animal's movement to or away from breeding grounds or feeding areas at certain times of year.

Mimic: to imitate or resemble something.

Nodosaurs: one of two types of Ankylosauria dinosaurs, nodosaurs had narrow heads, sideways-pointing spikes, and no club on their tails. (Compare with ANKYLOSAURS.)

Ornithischians: one of the two main groups of dinosaurs, these "bird-hipped" dinosaurs had hip bones that lay together behind the back leg.

Ornithopods: one of the three types of ornithischians, these dinosaurs ate plants, had beaklike mouths, probably stood on their back legs as well as all fours, and had three- or four-clawed toes.

Paleontology: the scientific study of fossils to learn more about past geologic periods.

Pangaea: a large landmass or supercontinent that formed during the Permian Period. It later broke apart, forming the continents that exist today.

Period: a division of geologic time (such as the Jurassic) that is longer than an epoch and is included in an era.

Predator: an animal that hunts other animals for food.

Prehistoric: the period of time before written history.

Prosauropods: a group of plant-eating dinosaurs that first appeared during the Triassic Period. Scientists think that they are related to the sauropods of a later period.

Reptile: a cold-blooded animal, usually covered with scales or bony plates, that slithers or crawls on its belly. Prehistoric reptiles sometimes flew or glided through the air, or swam in lakes or seas.

Saurischians: one of the two types of dinosaurs, these "lizard-hipped" dinosaurs had hips in which the two lower bones pointed in opposite directions.

Sauropods: "lizard-footed" dinosaurs, such as *Apatosaurus*, that ate plants, had long necks and tails, heavy bodies, short legs, and walked on all fours.

Scavenger: an animal, such as a vulture, that feeds on dead rather than live animals. *Dilophosaurus* was one of several dinosaur species that may have been scavengers.

Scutes: hard bony plates, such as those that cover the back of *Triceratops*.

Theropods: meat-eating dinosaurs, most of which had sharp teeth and claws; they walked on two feet, and were fast runners. *Tyrannosaurus* was a theropod.

Trackways: the fossilized footprints of dinosaurs, also called trace fossils because they are not part of an animal.

Wingspan: the distance from the tip of one of a pair of wings to the tip of the other.

Index

107

Picture Credits